W9-ARI-035

animalsanimals

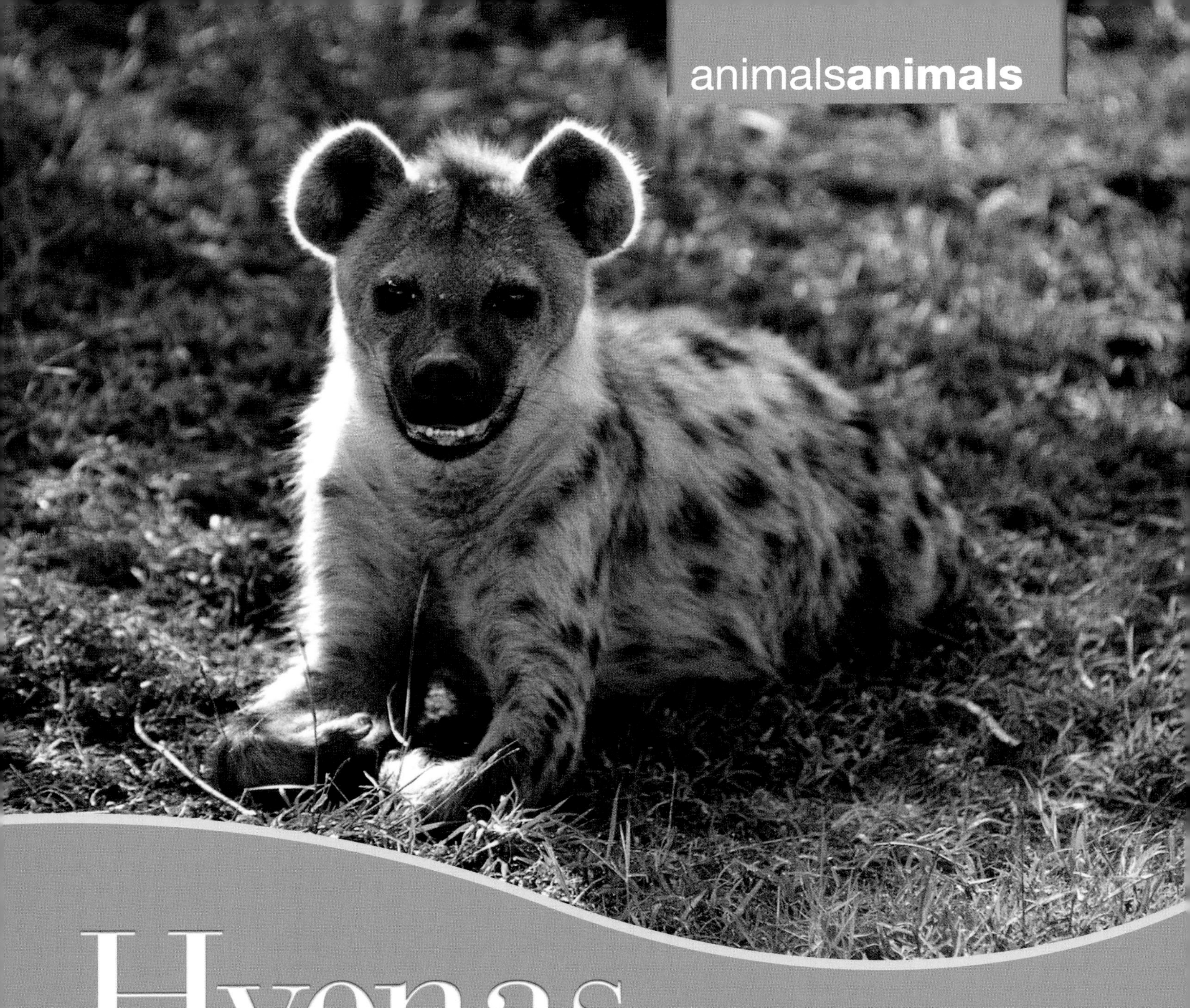

Hyenas

by **Gloria G. Schlaepfer**

Special thanks to Dr. Kay E. Holekamp, a professor in the Department of Zoology at Michigan State University, for her expert reading of this manuscript.

Thank you to my critique group—Laurie, Basia, and Karen—for your friendship, encouragement, and insight in the preparation of this manuscript.

Published by Marshall Cavendish Benchmark
An imprint of Marshall Cavendish Corporation

Other Marshall Cavendish Offices:
Marshall Cavendish International (Asia) Private Limited, 1 New Industrial Road, Singapore 536196 • Marshall Cavendish International (Thailand) Co Ltd. 253 Asoke, 12th Flr, Sukhumvit 21 Road, Klongtoey Nua, Wattana, Bangkok 10110, Thailand • Marshall Cavendish (Malaysia) Sdn Bhd, Times Subang, Lot 46, Subang Hi-Tech Industrial Park, Batu Tiga, 40000 Shah Alam, Selangor Darul Ehsan, Malaysia

Library of Congress Cataloging-in-Publication Data
Schlaepfer, Gloria G.
Hyenas / by Gloria G. Schlaepfer.
p. cm. — (Animals animals)
Includes index.
Summary: "Provides comprehensive information on the anatomy, special skills, habitats, and diet of hyenas"—Provided by publisher.
ISBN 978-0-7614-4838-9
1. Hyaenidae—Juvenile literature. I. Title.
QL737.C24S35 2011
599.74'3—dc22

2009022631

Photo research by Joan Meisel

Cover photo: James Hager/Getty Images

The photographs in this book are used by permission and through the courtesy of:
Alamy: blickwinkel, 6; Ann & Steve Toon, 18. *Corbis*: Terry Whittaker, Frank Lane Picture Agency; 20; Theo Allofs, 21; Yann Arthus-Bertrand, 22; Gallo Images, 32, 35, 40. *Getty Images:* DEA / F. Galardi, 1; Tim Graham, 4; Heinrich van den Berg, 7, 29; Beverly Joubert, 9, 13, 28; John & Barbara Gerlach, 10; Kim Wolhuter, 12, 41; Anup Shah, 15; Gerald Hinde, 27; Theo Allofs, 30; Kim Wolhuter, 33; Arthur Morris, 38. *Minden Pictures*: Kevin Schafer, 14; Suzi Eszterhas,16, 26; Anup Shah, 24; Terry Andrewartha/npl, 36.

Editor: Joy Bean
Publisher: Michelle Bisson
Art Director: Anahid Hamparian
Series Designer: Adam Mietlowski

Printed in Malaysia (T)
135642

Contents

1 Hunters and Scavengers

On the African **savanna**, the sun is bright and hot—too hot for the spotted hyenas to do anything more than lie around their den and doze. As the afternoon shadows lengthen and the sun drops below the horizon, a cooling breeze blows across the grassland and awakens the sleeping animals. With gaping yawns, they stand up and stretch their legs. Their sharp ears catch the soft murmurs carried by the wind from a distant herd of wildebeests. The hyenas are hungry. One by one, they leave the den site and sprint toward the grazing herd. More spotted hyenas join in, and the evening hunt begins. Hyenas are **carnivores**, and they are tough and clever animals.

During the hot afternoons on the savannas of Africa, hyenas rest.

The spotted hyena is one of four **species**, or types, belonging to a family of **mammals** called Hyaenidae. All four species can be found in Africa. The other species are the striped hyena, the brown hyena, and the aardwolf. The species are so different that one can easily tell them apart by their size, color of fur, and behavior.

The largest species is the spotted hyena, similar in size to a Great Dane. Irregularly shaped dark brown spots cover the spotted hyenas' yellow-brown, woolly fur and give them their name. Found in all parts of the African continent except in rain forests and the Sahara desert, spotted hyenas are the most numerous large carnivores on the continent. They outnumber lions many times over.

The spotted hyena is the largest of the four species of hyenas.

Whether in groups or alone, spotted hyenas are extremely capable hunters. One or two can kill a wildebeest, which weighs two to three times more than the hyenas do. As a team, they can run down a stocky zebra, a favorite meal.

Spotted hyenas are also **scavengers**; that is, they eat animals that are already dead. Nearly all carnivores, including lions and leopards, scavenge food

Wildebeests are big antelopes that roam in herds throughout the savannas. Hyenas hunt them for food.

whenever they can. Actually, hyenas eat whatever food is available and easiest to get.

The smaller striped and brown hyenas are similar in size to German shepherds. These two hyenas are primarily scavengers. When food is scarce, however, they will hunt small animals and insects, and even search out fruits and vegetables.

A powerful animal, the striped hyena is the only hyena that is found in Asia as well as in Africa. Numerous black stripes mark its grayish brown coat and long legs. Its large ears, nose, and throat are entirely black, while a thick mane of light-colored hair runs down its back. When the striped hyena is frightened or threatened, its mane stands straight up, like that of a scared house cat.

Did You Know . . .
Hyenas may resemble dogs a little, but the mongoose and the meerkat are the hyena's closest relatives.

Unlike its relatives, the brown hyena lives mainly in the dry, rocky scrubland of southwestern Africa. Sometimes it visits the Atlantic coast of Namibia, where it looks for dead seals and other marine animals. From that habit, the brown hyena earned the nickname beach wolf. It has a shaggy, dark brown coat of fur. A long, thick, white collar

The aardwolf is a type of hyena. It is recognizable by its large ears, pointed snout, and slender legs.

covers its neck and shoulders, and dark stripes line its legs.

The fourth type of hyena, the aardwolf, is a delicate, shy animal. It has a yellowish white coat of fur, with three vertical black stripes on the sides of its body. More black stripes encircle the animal's slender

In tropical savannas, the mounds, or above ground nests of termites, may be quite large.

legs. It can be distinguished from the other hyenas by its small size, weak jaws, and peglike molars.

The aardwolf's snout, or muzzle, is also long and pointed, which makes it easier for the animal to scoop up termites, its main food. In the Afrikaans language of South Africa, aardwolf means "earth wolf." It possibly got the name because it licks up the termites directly from their mound or off the ground.

Many people do not know the valuable roles hyenas play in Africa's ecosystem. Hyenas, as well as lions, wild dogs, and other **predators**, control the population of **prey** animals. In doing so, they help maintain the balance in nature. As scavengers, they are also nature's cleanup crew, helping in the decomposition, or decay, of the remains of dead animals.

Species Chart

- Spotted hyena

  Females: 147–165 pounds (67–75 kilograms)

  Males: 123–138 pounds (56–63 kg)

  30-36 inches (76–91 centimeters)

  Found in all habitats except rain forests and the Sahara desert

  Life span: 40 years in captivity

Spotted hyenas.

- Brown hyena
  77–110 pounds (35–50 kg)
  25–35 inches (64–89 cm)
  Lives mainly in the dry, rocky scrublands
  Life span: up to 13 years in captivity

A brown hyena.

- Striped hyena
  57–90 pounds (26–41 kg)
  26–29 inches (66–74 cm)
  Inhabits grasslands, bush, and stony, dry regions
  Life span: 20–25 years in captivity

A striped hyena.

- Aardwolf
  17–26 pounds (8–12 kg)
  15–20 inches (38–51 cm)
  Lives in open, dry savannas and farmlands
  Life span: 15 years in captivity

An aardwolf.

2 Mom Rules

Known as fearsome predators, spotted hyenas show another side to their personalities when they settle into complex social groups, called **clans**. The alpha female is the highest-ranking female of her clan, which contains multiple families. A **matriarch**, the oldest and highest-ranking female, heads each family. Clan members come together at kills, to defend the clan's **territory**, and at a communal den.

No two clans are alike. In East Africa there are great herds of antelopes, the main prey of spotted hyenas. There is plenty of food to feed thirty-five to eighty hyenas in one clan. But in the Kalahari Desert of southern Africa, prey animals are scarce. That

A mother hyena takes good care of her pups. Here she keeps them safe in their den.

means less food; and clan sizes are smaller, with as few as twelve members.

Life for the clan centers on the den. It is where hyenas hang out and cubs are raised. Since spotted hyenas are combative, even with one another, they manage to keep the peace within the clan by using a ranking order. Each hyena knows its rank, its place in

The capture of a prey animal brings clan members to the feast.

the clan's **hierarchy**. The **alpha female** is at the top. Her cubs and close relatives rank steps below her. The matriarchs and other female members of the clan are below them, with males at the bottom. To challenge a higher-ranking hyena could mean a vicious fight.

The other hyena species live in noticeably different kinds of groups. Brown hyenas form small clans of related females, their male mates, and cubs. The highest-ranking female and male are of equal status.

Striped hyenas live in small family clusters: a female and two to three males or a mated pair and their offspring. They rest together during the day, but each animal forages alone at night.

The most solitary hyena is the aardwolf. Only after a pair has mated and cubs are born do the male and female share a den and hunting territory.

Hyenas have keen senses of eyesight, hearing, and smell. They spot prey using their eyes and ears. They can smell the rotting flesh of meat, or **carrion**, from far away.

Their sense of smell also tells them what is happening in their world. From the sac beneath their tail, called the **anal pouch**,

Did You Know. . .

All hyenas have long, powerful necks, well-developed upper bodies, and long front legs. Their hind legs, however, are shorter, giving them their distinctive sloping back and bearlike walk.

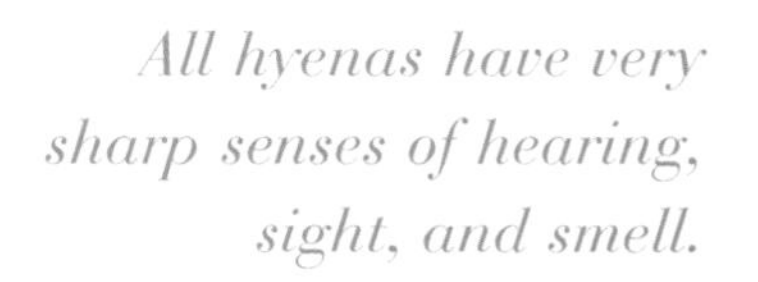

All hyenas have very sharp senses of hearing, sight, and smell.

hyenas eject a strong-smelling yellowish paste. They target blades of grass or twigs. The scent of the paste is unique to each animal and relays a message to other hyenas passing by that says, "I was here." Clans also mark the boundaries of their large territories with the yellowish paste. It is a warning to a neighboring clan not to cross over the border or it will risk a fight.

Hyenas also use body language and their sense of touch to communicate. When they meet after being separated, hyenas engage in elaborate greeting ceremonies. Striped hyenas sniff each other's mid back, nose, and turned-out anal pouch.

A low ranking hyena crouches with its tail between its legs and grimaces when meeting a higher ranking clan member.

Brown hyenas crouch and present themselves to one another. The lower-ranking animal holds its ears back and grins, exposing its teeth. Sometimes the **dominant** brown hyena grabs hold of a lower-ranking animal with its teeth and shakes its neck and throat. Scientists think these **rituals** strengthen the clan's hierarchy and its ability to get along without fighting. Unlike the other hyena species, the aardwolf has no special greeting rituals. Of all the hyenas, spotted hyenas are the most vocal. They giggle, growl, groan,

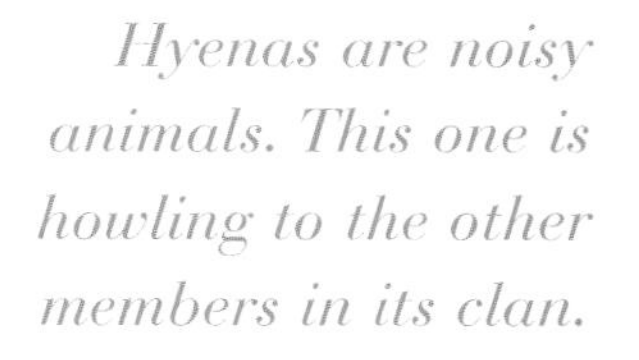

Hyenas are noisy animals. This one is howling to the other members in its clan.

whoop, and even scream. The high, cackling giggle is not actually laughter but rather an expression of intense excitement or fear. Their whooping noise is a direct call to other clan members. The *o-o-o-o* rises slowly and loudly. It ends with a low *o-o-o-o-o*. Whoops carry for miles; and with each repetition, listeners learn the caller's location. Whoops can be a call for others to join the feast or a rallying cry to protect the clan's border.

Brown and striped hyenas are less vocal than their spotted cousins. They do growl and emit soft howls, however, as do the still quieter aardwolves.

3 Den Mothers

Among hyenas, mating can take place throughout the year. A male spotted hyena knows when a female is ready to mate, and he also knows how to approach her. He does so carefully. Standing a few feet behind her, he watches patiently. Without making a sound, he bows his head until his chin touches the ground. He rises, then he moves closer, bows again, and paws the ground near her. If the female shows any hostility toward him, he retreats immediately.

Other males may arrive and drive off the first suitor. The female is in charge, and she decides which male will be the father of her cubs. After they mate, the male does not hang around but wanders off to look for another likely partner.

Hyenas go through elaborate greeting rituals when meeting.

Four months later, the female spotted hyena finds an abandoned **burrow** that will be big enough for her and her newborn twin cubs. She stays with them for the first days of their lives. They are roly-poly balls of black fur. Unlike the eyes of newborn kittens and puppies, the gray-blue eyes of spotted hyena cubs are open; and the cubs have mouths full of sharp teeth.

Soon after birth, the cubs show the natural aggressiveness of spotted hyenas when they begin to fight. They bite each other's neck and shoulders until the stronger cub is accepted as the dominant one.

When the cubs are about a month old, the spotted hyena mother transfers them to a communal den. Amazingly, the hyena, whose powerful jaws can crunch bones and tear zebra hide, carries her tiny cubs in her mouth without injuring them. In the den,

A thirty-four-day-old cub rests with its mother.

the cubs grow up with other cubs of different ages. By four months of age their baby fur has taken on the spotted coat of an adult.

When the cubs are small, their mother lies outside the cramped burrow and calls to them with soft, groaning sounds to suckle. She nurses only her own cubs. Her milk is their main source of food for the next year or more. Spotted hyenas seldom carry back food to the den for their young.

Mother hyenas are very protective of their cubs. They snap at other hyenas and chase them away from the den site. Lions and eagles prey on the young hyenas. At the first sign of danger,

Did You Know . . .

Female spotted hyenas look so much like males that ordinary people cannot tell them apart. Often it is only after a female gives birth that her sex becomes clear.

At about six weeks of age, the fur of a spotted hyena cub begins to lighten. By nine months, it has its adult spots.

though, the cubs scoot into the den and remain quietly motionless.

Early life is a little different for the brown and striped hyenas. They give birth to two to four fluffy cubs after a three-month **gestation** period, or the time it takes babies to develop inside their mother. The cubs are helpless for seven to nine days because their eyes are sealed. The mother visits the den several times a day to nurse them.

Brown hyena cubs depend completely on their mother's milk for three to four months. By then they are eating solid food. Their need for milk, though, continues for ten to fifteen more months. Unlike a spotted hyena mother, a female brown hyena will nurse infants that

Spotted hyenas usually give birth to twin cubs.

Two aardwolf pups stick together as they head out of their den.

are not her own; and both males and females carry food back to the den for the youngsters.

In contrast, a striped hyena mother does not get support from others. She cares for her cubs all alone. Mothers nurse their cubs for a year, even though they take back solid food to the den for them.

During spring or fall, the male aardwolf searches his territory for a female to mate with. Gestation lasts for about ninety days. The female aardwolf gives birth to two or three cubs. The helpless cubs spend their first six to eight weeks in the den. During that time, the male may stay near the den opening at night while the mother forages for food. The cubs develop rapidly. By three months they can follow a parent on his or her nightly rounds in the search for termites. At four months the independent cubs hunt alone for termites. Eventually the young aardwolves wander off to set up their own territories.

4 From Antelopes to Termites

When spotted hyenas eat, they devour their food rapidly. They growl, push, and shove one another to get hunks of meat. It is a food frenzy—bloody and noisy. Often, lions hear them and rush to seize control of the **carcass**. A brief fight ensues before the hyenas slink away. They may return after the lions leave in order to pick over the bones and look for meat scraps. In Africa, theft of food is common. Lions steal from hyenas, and hyenas steal from lions and other carnivores.

Because spotted hyenas are such excellent hunters, they kill most of the food they eat. Packs of hyenas use their intelligence and speed to take down a large prey animal such as a wildebeest or zebra. Typically, one or

Hyenas and lions compete directly for food. They often scavenge from each others kills.

two hyenas head toward a grazing herd together. The prey animals continue to eat as they keep a watchful eye on the predators. Suddenly, the hyenas dash into the herd, causing their prey to flee in panic. If one animal runs more slowly than the others, the hyenas choose it and give chase.

More clan members join the hunt. Working as a team, they outwit and outrun the victim. If caught, the wildebeest or zebra provides food for all the hunters. When hyenas eat, they are not fussy—and nothing is wasted. A hungry pack can reduce a 992-pound (450-kg) zebra to a pile of hooves and clumps of hide and hair in thirty minutes. Hyenas crack open bones that lions and leopards cannot crush and then dig out the nutritious **marrow**.

Did You Know . . .
The ancestors of present-day hyenas, *Pachycrocuta brevirostris*, were as large as lions. They had powerful jaws and humongous teeth that could easily splinter the massive leg bones of a rhinoceros or mammoth.

Brown and striped hyenas do not chase large game or hunt in packs. They are mainly scavengers, eating and digesting parts of prey animals left by other predators. It is not easy being a scavenger, though. Carrion is widely scattered, and the animals spend long nights searching for it. Striped and brown hyenas locate carcasses mostly by

Zebras graze calmly as a hyena guards its kill.

scent. When carrion is scarce, the hyenas' diet changes. They add insects, birds' eggs, small mammals such as mice, and anything they can catch to ease their hunger. In dry weather, the hyenas may raid farmers' fields and take melons, a good source of water.

In the desert, semidesert, and coastal terrains where brown hyenas live, food is particularly difficult to find. They must scavenge from the kills of lions and other carnivores. In their nightly searches, brown hyenas may travel more than 19 square miles (49 square kilometers). When the hyena finds food, it often hides the scraps in a hole or clump of grass to keep it from being stolen. The next night the hyena returns to eat the remains. If its den is within a few miles and the carcass is small, a brown hyena will carry the bones back to the den to feed the cubs. A feast for these hyenas is finding a dead seal on the beach.

A striped hyena also patrols its territory at night in search of food. The well-marked hyena is hard to spot as it moves noiselessly through tall grass and bushes. The striped hyena listens for sounds from other predators and uses its very keen sense of smell to locate carrion.

Other animals may find the carcass too. The striped hyena is not aggressive, however, and does not challenge intruders. It pulls back and waits. Many times the bones are all that is left. That is not a problem for the hyena.

Three brown hyenas raid an ostrich nest.

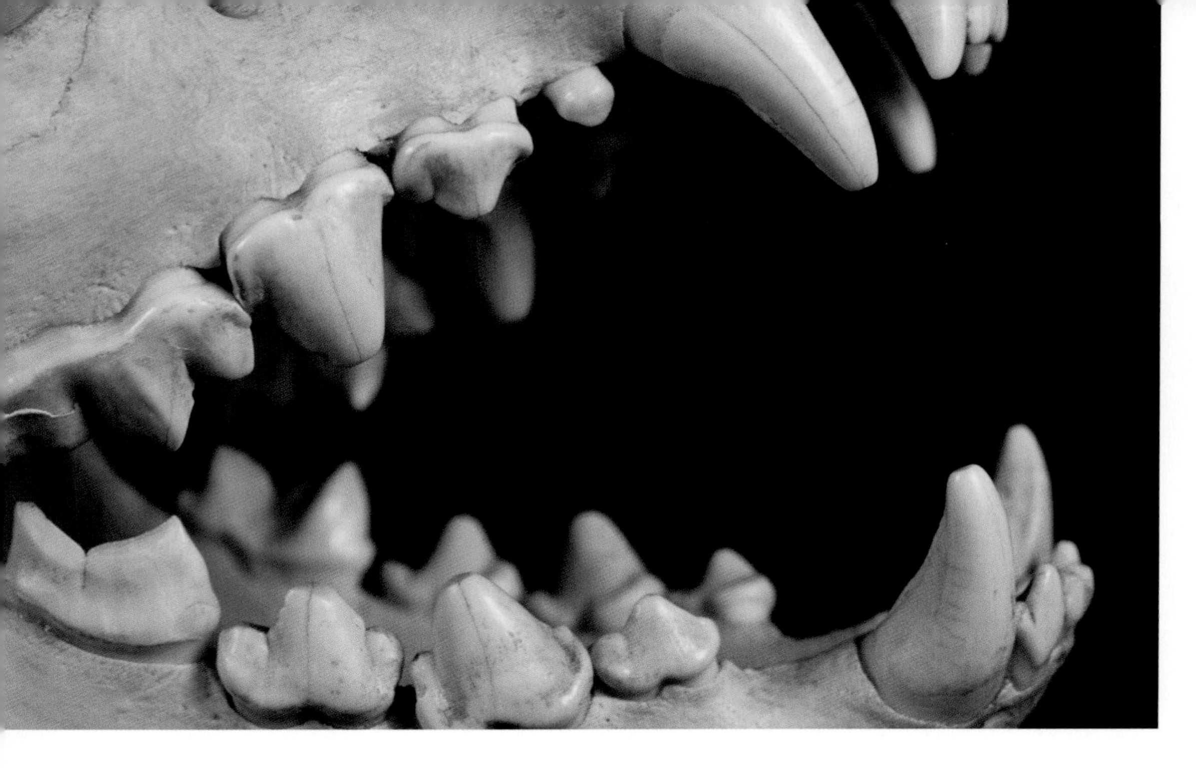

The teeth of a hyena are very strong and they can crush bones with no trouble at all.

With its massive jaws and strong teeth, it can crush, swallow, and digest all uneaten parts of the carcass.

Unlike the other types of hyenas, the aardwolf specializes in eating insects, mainly harvester termites. The termites depend on dry grass and wood for food and are most numerous on grasslands and savannas grazed by hoofed animals. The insects emerge at night to feed. The aardwolf easily licks up the long columns of five thousand or more insects by using its long, sticky tongue. Other termite-eating mammals avoid the insects because of the disagreeable chemicals that the **soldier termites** secrete. The aardwolf can digest the chemicals without harm to itself.

5 A Dangerous Life

Carnivores are not vicious or angry. They kill their prey only in order to eat. To hunt successfully, carnivores must learn how a prey animal behaves and watch for physical weaknesses. They must use skill, speed, patience, and strength to catch a prey species.

Individual spotted hyenas will hunt small animals, but the teamwork of a pack is most successful in bringing down a large animal. Spotted hyenas, lions, leopards, and wild dogs hunt the same prey animals. Whichever carnivore is the fastest and smartest gets its dinner first.

The speed of wild dogs gives them an advantage over hyenas. Hyenas sometimes follow the dogs and

A pack of hyenas can chase a lion from a kill.

brazenly try to steal meat from them. But the dogs bite the intruding hyenas' rumps until they back off.

Hyenas and vultures have a special relationship. The soaring birds can easily spot hyenas at a kill and join them, squabbling for the choicest cuts. At other times, the tables are turned when spotted hyenas watch vultures descend to earth. Hoping for a meal, the hyenas race to find the carcass.

Contact between lions and spotted hyenas can be hostile, and often an encounter turns violent. The bitterness between them goes beyond competition for food. In films and reports from naturalists, the two predators are seen as deadly enemies, ready to challenge each other and fight. Male lions are even known to actively hunt down and kill a hyena but not eat it.

While spotted hyenas normally hunt at dusk and in the early morning hours, brown and striped hyenas

Vultures often fly above the site where hyenas have made a kill. The vultures will swoop in, trying to snatch a piece of the meal.

generally forage alone for carrion throughout the night. They are not the only **nocturnal** scavengers, however. A large carcass will attract a swarm of species including jackals, vultures, foxes, wild dogs, spotted hyenas, and lions. Feeding disputes are common. Brown and striped hyenas will work to defend their food find, but large predators usually take over. Unlike the other hyenas, the shy, nocturnal aardwolf is a massive killer of termites, lapping up a good meal of 200,000 or more of them a night. At times, the aardwolf gets help from another **insectivore** that shares its habitat: the aardvark. With its strong claws, the aardwolf easily breaks the hard crust of a termite mound. Then both animals will feast.

Many farmers consider aardwolves useful because termites damage crops and buildings, so the insectivores may receive protection from them. Other farmers, though, suspect them of killing lambs, and they trap or shoot the aardwolves. In addition, black-backed jackals, lions, and other types of hyenas prey upon aardwolves.

Hyenas cannot seem to shake their bad reputation. Many people in Africa do not like

Did You Know . . .

Zoologist Dr. Kay Holekamp and her colleagues have been studying spotted hyenas in Kenya for twenty-five years. They track the animals from birth to death to learn how hyenas behave in their complex society. "It's like following a soap opera," says Dr. Holekamp.

An aardwolf licks a trail of termites directly from the soil surface, eating as many as 200,000 termites or more a night.

hyenas, either because the hyenas eat carrion or because they believe false stories that hyenas rob graves, snatch children, or change into werewolves. People do not like or trust hyenas near their villages. The animals continue to be shot, poisoned, trapped, and snared regularly because they kill local cows, sheep, and sometimes humans. Killing of hyenas even takes place within protected areas, or preserves; but most often it occurs near farms and ranches after the slaughter of domestic animals.

As large predators, hyenas present a challenge to biologists. These scientists are looking for ways to help humans overcome their strong negative feelings toward these animals and, at the same time, protect them. Many believe that teaching children and adults about wildlife and its place in the natural world is a good first step. As well, Africans must continue to find new ways to shelter their livestock from roaming predators.

Hyenas are fascinating animals. They are not savage killers. Nor are they wimpy, slobbering cowards as portrayed in the popular Disney movie *The Lion King*. That exaggeration keeps alive misinformation about these intelligent predators.

Perhaps sometime in the future people will recognize hyenas for what they are: strong, smart, and social mammals that are vital members of the African ecosystem.

Hyenas have been proven to be social animals. Here, a curious hyena investigates a photographer in South Africa.

Glossary

alpha female—The highest ranking member of a clan.

anal pouch—The sac located beneath the tail.

burrow (noun)—A hole or tunnel in the ground made by an animal as a place to live and feel safe.

carcass—The body of a dead animal.

carnivore—An animal that feeds on the flesh of other animals.

carrion—The decaying flesh of a dead animal.

clan—A group of individuals or entire families that share a den and defend a common territory.

dominant—Ruling, or controlling; having or showing authority or influence.

gestation—The period of time it takes a baby to develop inside its mother.

hierarchy—The relationship among animals of the same species in which one ranks above the other, giving it greater access to food, mates, or denning sites.

insectivore—An animal that feeds on insects.

mammal—A warm-blooded animal that is covered with hair or fur, gives birth to live young, and feeds them milk by nursing.

marrow—The soft, fatty substance that fills the hollow parts of bones.

matriarch—A female that heads a family.

nocturnal—To be active at night.

predator—An animal that hunts and eats another animal (prey).

prey—An animal that is hunted and eaten by another animal (predator).

ritual—Any pattern of behavior regularly performed in a set manner.

savanna—A grassy environment with few trees found in hot, dry climates.

scavenger—An animal or other organism that feeds on dead organic matter.

soldier termites—The protectors of a termite colony.

species—A group of individuals having some common characteristics.

territory—An area that an animal defends as its own for finding food, and raising young.

Find Out More

Books

Malam, John. *Hyenas*. New York: Franklin Watts, 2008.

Websites

Answers to questions children ask about hyenas
www.hyaenidae.org/just-for-kids.html

Denver Zoo
www.denverzoo.org/animals/spottedHyena.asp

San Diego Zoo
www.sandiegozoo.org/animalbytes/t-striped_hyena.html

Index

Page numbers for illustrations are in **boldface**.

About the Author

Gloria G. Schlaepfer is the author of seven nonfiction books for elementary school children, with a focus on wild animals. Mrs. Schlaepfer has been an environmental educator with Project Learning Tree and the San Joaquin Wildlife Sanctuary.

She enjoys gardening, photography, and worldwide traveling. The mother of four grown children and grandmother of four grandchildren, she lives with her husband, Karl Schlaepfer, in Fullerton, California.